YOU ARE BRAVE

WRITTEN BY TODD SNOW
ILLUSTRATED BY MELODEE STRONG

Maren Green Publishing, Inc.
Oak Park Heights, Minnesota

FOR MEREDY,
BECAUSE YOU ARE.
-T.S.

TO MY LITTLE SIS,
FOR BEING BRAVE IN SO MANY WAYS.
I AM SO PROUD OF YOU!
LOVE, MELODEE

Ages 4 and up

Maren Green Publishing, Inc.
5630 Memorial Avenue North, Suite 3
Oak Park Heights, MN 55082
Toll-free 800-287-1512

Library of Congress Cataloging-in-Publication Data is available.

Edited by Pamela Espeland

Text set in Garamond Pro and Wonderlism
Illustrations created using acrylic on wood

First Edition November 2008
10 9 8 7 6 5 4 3 2
Manufactured in Shenzhen, Guangdong, China - 0615

ISBN 978-1-934277-19-5 (pbk.)

www.marengreen.com

YOU ARE BRAVE

IN MANY WAYS.

YOU ARE BRAVE WHEN
YOU CLIMB HIGH

AND SLIDE FAST.

YOU ARE BRAVE WHEN
YOU LET FRIENDS

PLAY WITH YOUR TOYS.

AND ASK
THE OWNER
IF YOU CAN
PET IT.

YOU ARE BRAVE WHEN YOU FIND A BUG

AND HOLD IT GENTLY.

AND YOU SAY "GOOD-BYE."

YOU ARE BRAVE
WHEN YOU TRY A NEW FOOD

EVEN IF
YOU'RE NOT
SURE YOU'LL
LIKE IT.

YOU ARE BRAVE
WHEN IT'S DARK

AND TIME FOR BED.
(NIGHT-NIGHT, SLEEP TIGHT!)

Also available from Maren Green Publishing

ISBN 978-1-934277-18-8

You Are Friendly *By Todd Snow, illustrated by Melodee Strong.* Children want to make friends and be friendly. This warm, affirming book helps them build important social skills. Sharing, saying "please" and "thank you," inviting others to join in and play, treating people and animals kindly, and offering to help are all ways to win friends. Written in simple words, vividly illustrated with realistic scenes that relate to children's everyday lives, *You Are Friendly* guides children to create healthy, positive relationships with others. *Paperback, full color, 8" x 8", 24 pages. Ages 4 & up.* MG120 **$8.99**

Also available in board book format: Full color, 6" x 6", 24 pages, Ages Baby—Preschool. (ISBN 978-1-934277-09-6) MG109 **$6.99**

You Are Healthy *By Todd Snow, illustrated by Melodee Strong.* Experts have identified key behaviors important to children's health. These include active play, eating right, washing hands, drinking water, getting enough sleep, and spending time with loved ones. This warm, inviting book introduces young children to things they can do to stay healthy and happy. Written in simple words, vividly illustrated with realistic scenes that relate to children's everyday lives, *You Are Healthy* is an ideal introduction to a lifetime of good health. *Paperback, full color, 8" x 8", 24 pages. Ages 4 & up.* MG117 **$8.99**

ISBN 978-1-934277-22-5

ISBN 978-1-934277-23-2

You Are Helpful *By Todd Snow, illustrated by Melodee Strong.* Children want to be helpful and are eager to become more independent. We see this whenever children insist "I can do it myself!" or "Let me!" This warm, inviting book introduces young children to age-appropriate ways to help out: put their toys away, get dressed by themselves, wait their turn, sit still at the doctor's office. Written in simple words, vividly illustrated with realistic scenes that relate to children's everyday lives, *You Are Helpful* lets children know they are competent and capable. *Paperback, full color, 8" x 8", 24 pages. Ages 4 & up.* MG118 **$8.99**

w w w . m a r e n g r e e n . c o m

5525 Memorial Avenue North, Suite 6 • Oak Park Heights, MN 55082
phone 800-287-1512 • 651-439-4500 • fax 651-439-4532 • email orders@marengreen.com